# RED STAR OVER CUBA

# RED STAR OVER CUBA

by Don Crawford
and Brother Andrew

Inside story by "God's Smuggler" and
Christian refugees from Communism

TYNDALE HOUSE PUBLISHERS
Wheaton, Illinois

Coverdale House Publishers, Ltd., London, England

Library of Congress Catalog Card Number 76-123286
SBN 8423-5350-X

**Third printing, August 1971**

Printed in the United States of America.

To Clareta
and the Five

## ACKNOWLEDGEMENTS

The author is indebted to many persons who sacrificed much that this book might be written. For security reasons the names of some cannot be published. However, for their special contributions, the following must be mentioned:

BROTHER ANDREW, who has long masked his own identity in bringing Bibles and hope to Christians in Communist countries, for telling his own story of recent visits to Cuba as well as permitting the use of a few incidents previously recorded in *God's Smuggler* (with John and Elizabeth Sherrill, the New American Library, 1967).

HERBERT and MARJORIE CAUDILL, missionaries for forty years to the island of Cuba, for invaluable technical assistance in the preparation of the manuscript.

DOMINGO FERNANDEZ, whose U.S.-based radio ministry is reaching and encouraging Christians still suffering in Cuba, for illuminating background information about the Church there.

JUAN ROJAS, himself a former Cuban, for arranging numerous interviews with refugees in Miami, acting as interpreter, and performing a second-mile service for the author.

# CONTENTS

*Russia's Premier Nikita Khrushchev and Fidel Castro at historic meeting in New York in 1960. They were in town to attend the U.N. General Assembly meeting and to let the world know that new bonds existed between Cuba and the U.S.S.R.*

UPI Roto Service photo

## PREVIEW

"It's easy to get to Cuba," went the quip. "Just take any jet to Miami . . . most of them have a stopover in Havana."

The joke had lost most of its humor by 1971, for airline hijackings to the tiny island republic off the tip of Florida remind Americans of the proximity of a hostile Communist nation — and the loss of an amiable neighbor and delightful vacation resort. Getting into Cuba has not been easy for American travelers since governmental relations were severed in 1961. *Bona fide* visits to Cuba are comparatively rare, deterred by the United States' ban on regular travel to the island and Cuba's reluctance to grant visas to Americans. The Rev. Clifton Fite spent nearly two years, from 1965 until 1967, on an international bureaucratic runaround just to get the proper credentials for a humanitarian journey to see his son in a Cuban prison. In contrast, unauthorized visits by avowedly anti-American Americans seem easily accomplished. U.S. revolutionaries find their way into Cuba via a mutually recognized nation, such as Canada, Mexico, or Spain. It was by way of Mexico that groups organized by the Black Panthers and Students for a Democratic Society went to "help in the sugarcane harvest" in 1969 and 1970 — while actually studying guerrilla warfare.

This book suggests another way to reach — and aid — Cuba. The proposed avenue is a journey of the mind with guidance from Cubans who have lived there and loved their land. The aid to Cuba will be transmitted by prayer over a bridge of accurate knowledge about Cuba and the living promise of God in James 5:16 that "the effectual fervent prayer of a righteous man availeth much." Effectual prayer is urgently needed for Cuba, and it is engendered by a compassionate knowledge of real needs. To this end the author has interviewed a number of Cuban refugees who fled their beleaguered land and still long and pray for justice and freedom for their compatriots to worship God. Each chapter presents the story of one of these brave Christians.

I am grateful for Brother Andrew's contribution to this goal of enlisting prayer support, through his introductory report on things seen, heard, and felt during his 1969 visit to Cuba. As demonstrated in his thrilling book, *God's Smuggler,* this daring Dutchman recognizes only the barricades erected by

God — even in Cuba. And he has proved the only barricades to prayer are self-made.

Don Crawford
Carol Stream, Illinois

*Chapter One*

# "GOD'S SMUGGLER" IN CUBA

Cuba, a year later . . . a year later . . . a year later . . . every time we visit Cuba we see that the situation has become more difficult — the standard of living has fallen, courage has ebbed, the pressure on the churches has increased.

To be honest, we have wondered how long the people will tolerate all this, whether they will rebel and throw off the yoke. But as Cuba's poor masses now have more medical care, education, and recognition than under Batista, a revolt may never come.

Such questions, however, were not our prime concern. We had been sent with a message of encouragement from the Lord: "To strengthen what remains and is on the point of death" (Revelation 3:2).

Fortunately, we had quite a lot with which to strengthen the brethren. To begin with, very practical things ranged from razor blades to vitamin pills, and there was quite a lot more for families of those who are in prison for the sake of the gospel. But the greatest thing was our simply being there as a messenger from the Lord, with a message of the Kingdom of God and his righteousness.

Compared with previous years, there were not so many Christian leaders in prison at the time of this visit, though it is still very easy to land there.

One of my friends had just been released from prison, where he had spent six months. His "crime" was that he had prayed with a member of his congregation when visiting his house. During this prayer the secret police had entered and arrested him.

Why are there fewer Christian leaders in prison at the moment? Perhaps because the whole country is more like a prison. The land is divided into many small sections, so that even every street is divided into what is called a CDR: *Comitee Defensa de la Revolucion* (Committee for the Defense of the Revolution). The members of each committee watch the buildings and houses in their section and track down any counterrevolutionaries.

During the first year after the revolution, 100,000 of these committees were set up, and the number has steadily grown. So it is possible for the State to know what happens inside houses, even when a minister goes in to pray with someone.

These committees also arrange the "reception services" in every street where there is a church building. They provide an alternative "program" to attract children away from the church. Young people who enter the churches are listed as potential enemies of the State. All Christian activities are hindered in this way.

During my first journey to Cuba, Christian leaders often asked me what their attitude should be to the authorities. I believe that Christians can live under any kind of government, because socialism, for example, is not necessarily more ungodly than a capitalist system. The Christians' reactions depend on what demands are made on them, what degree of freedom they have to differ with State policies, and what the Bible situation is.

When I ponder the nature of atheistic Communism, however, my thoughts revert to Amalek in the Bible. In Deuteronomy 25:17, 18 we read that his tactics were to cut off the defenseless ones in Israel, the slow individuals consisting of old people, women, and children — and Amalek did not fear God. Cuba's persecution is fierce against the Christians and is directed at the weak and the children. This antagonism is spiritual more than physical, and the victory must be spiritual.

Before 1969 there was considerable optimism in Cuba about the Bible situation. The Bible shop was still open, negotiations continued with Bible societies abroad for shipments, and delay seemed to be the only obstacle to Bible distribution. But after years of promises and excuses, the Bible shop has been finally closed.

Casual visitors to Cuba have thought Bibles were

available — after all, there was one in the shop
window. Yes, but the shelves inside were empty,
the drawers were full of orders — and clerks were
forbidden to sell the one Bible in the window. Also,
the Bibles which arrived in Cuba in small parcels
were — and still are — destroyed.

Another attack upon the Church is in the guise
of the so-called ecumenical movement. By bringing
smaller, independent groups into an island-wide
council of churches the government keeps tabs on
the number of members and names of the leaders.

Low wages restrict the ministry of some pastors.
The average wage in Cuba is about twenty-two
pesos ($22) a week, that of a doctor is a hundred
pesos, and the pastor of a small church gets only
twelve pesos. This is not the case, however, for
ministers of the Baptist, Anglican, Methodist, and
Presbyterian churches, who receive more. With all
food rationed, one needs a lot of money to obtain
supplementary food. To supply their families with
more than the bare minimum, pastors have to work
long hours outside their churches.

Apparently the Christians were not prepared for
these difficult times. Man has the capacity to survive under the most hostile conditions, but my heart
breaks to see such conditions in Cuba, in both material and spiritual terms.

At the World Congress on Evangelism in Berlin
I met some American missionaries who had built
up a flourishing work in Cuba. But one of them
told me, with tears in his eyes, "When we had to

withdraw from Cuba, we did not leave any leaders behind."

Christians can lack many things and survive, but if there is a lack of vision and leadership, then, says the Bible, "the people perish." Cuba's great problem is lack of spiritual leaders.

A few Bible schools were still functioning when I visited, but not that of the Assemblies of God, a large group in Cuba. Their seminary has long been shut, as are thirty percent of their smaller churches. They have a sort of evening Bible school at the church in Havana where about forty members meet almost every evening for study.

I spoke there several times to the students, and they had invited other members of the church to attend also. The first evening my interpreter almost collapsed after about an hour and had to sit down. We continued with another interpreter, then on the ride back to the hotel the first interpreter explained why he was so tired. The previous day he had received a message that a parcel had arrived at the station for him. His mother, who lives in farm country, had sent him some extra food. To get the package, he had to stand in line for eight hours without food or drink. No wonder he was exhausted.

Other Bible schools have between ten and twenty students. Young people attend who have counted the cost, and they need our prayers. Among them are a number who committed themselves to full-time service on my previous visits to the island. So

I feel particularly responsible for some of them, and would like to share that responsibility with praying Christians.

As I preached to people in Cuba, I saw longing eyes, hungry hearts, and many sick in body. Pastors asked me to speak about healing and the full armor of the Holy Spirit. It is no wonder that so many are sick: a doctor told me that perhaps only ten of every hundred patients for whom they write prescriptions manage to buy medicines.

Many appear to be mentally sick, especially among the children. I saw them sitting in the meetings, sick and undernourished, and talked with some after the services. In one service I gave an invitation to the sick for prayers and more than two hundred came forward. The Lord gave much grace, and there was much faith and power for healing. We saw miracles. I had the feeling: God *must* do it here, for there is so much need.

Where there is so much need, God will work great miracles. We saw this at the annual conference of the Church of the Nazarene. One Sunday morning we were drawn out of the meeting by a group of excited people urging, "A man is possessed; come and help us quickly."

As we walked about two hundred yards across a field, groups of children ran toward us in terror. When we arrived, we saw a short, slim man, with dark hair and a moustache, fighting with at least ten men. He threw them to the ground with supernatural power, roaring at them and rolling his eyes wildly.

Bystanders were praying, calling on the name of Jesus and pleading the power of his blood.

Soon the man calmed down sufficiently to be laid on a stretcher. I went up to him then and commanded the demons to leave him, laying my hands on him and praying for him. Great was the joy of those at the conference when this man gave a testimony to his Lord in a youth meeting that evening. The end of that conference was glorious.

The Methodist bishop spoke at the last meeting. His theme was taken from Ephesians 6: the spiritual armor of God. An Orthodox priest who was present had told me earlier that ordinary weapons are not much good against Communism. "We have got to learn to use spiritual weapons," he said. "At least three times a day I pray, binding the powers of atheism and fighting against the powers of darkness in the air."

His words agreed with the message of the Methodist bishop. "We are not contending against flesh and blood," he said, and quietly he gave a biblical message about the whole armor of God. The armor lies ready; all we have to do is put it on. If anyone does not do that, he cannot fight in the way God wishes us to. Either we cannot see the enemy, or, through lack of the proper equipment, we attack an enemy that we cannot handle in our own weakness, and so we do not win a single battle, far less the war.

The Cuban revolution is aimed at changing not only society, but the people themselves. Che Guevera said, "If our revolution is not aimed at changing people, then I am not interested." I read the same theme in many Cuban books and papers: We are engaged in developing a new race of people.

This thought oppresses me, for the change is away from God. In a junior school in Havana not long ago, the teacher spoke directly against God. He persuasively explained that it is old-fashioned to believe in God in this enlightened age. Then he asked any child who still believed in God to stand up. Just one girl stood up, a thirteen-year-old girl I know personally. I have tried to imagine the situation as if I were that girl; it stirred me deeply, and I thought of the dark future of this people and other peoples in Communist countries.

Christians, too, aim at a new race of men, a new kind of person, born spiritually by faith in Jesus Christ. Wherever the preaching of the Christian message is not allowed — and this happens in non-Communist countries also — there is a conflict which challenges the total commitment of the Christian, a commitment which can cost one's life, a commitment which has already cost the lives of thousands who preceded us.

While saying good-bye to a pastor at the airport, my missionary colleague and I gave him something from our now meager supply of goods. He was lost for words to thank us. Finally he said, "One day you will give your lives for us; you have given us everything you had and you have nothing else to give."

I could not help but ponder his words as our Cuban Airlines plane flew toward Mexico and to freedom. I could still hear the questions, the complaints, the longings, the stammering, the thanks . . . and I remembered the thrilling words:

"Let that attitude which inspired Christ Jesus rule you: he did not cling to his rights; he emptied himself; he humbled himself to be obedient even to death, therefore God has exalted him and given him a name which is above every name, so that all who dwell in heaven, and earth, and hell should bow the knee to the name of Jesus, and every tongue confess to the glory of God the Father — Jesus Christ is Lord" (Philippians 2:5-11, English rendering of the Dutch Willibrord version).

*—Brother Andrew*

*Happy reunion of unidentified refugees at the Miami airport.*

*Chapter Two*

## CREEPING DISEASE

As Maria stepped from the Rosales home into the warm spring evening, she looked back at her mother, hoping for some sign of blessing on her venture. Her mother's wave told Maria all was well. The daughter was departing from her expected performance as a senior at Santa Margarita High School, in attending services at a Protestant church, but her mother seemed to understand the girl's quest for deeper meaning in her faith. Earlier, she had sanctioned Maria's attendance at a Sunday morning Bible class in the little mission. Maria herself had been apprehensive at the time. Her friend Juanita, however, had been so enthusiastic about the class for high school girls that Maria had decided to attend just once.

Maria was surprised to learn that the sacred Bible could be a guidebook for problems of a modern age, even those Cuba faced in 1957. It was exciting to learn how Christianity had transcended the troubles of the world, and whatever the import of the uprising launched recently by Fidel Castro in Oriente Province or the effect of the brutal counterrevolution by President Batista — the faith would endure. The teacher of the class skillfully used newspaper clippings and Bible references to make the study not only interesting but meaningful. So Maria had become a regular attendant. When the teacher announced that an *americano* would speak at a special midweek meeting, Maria and Juanita had decided to go, not really knowing what an "evangelistic" meeting was.

Americans were no novelty in a resort city like Havana, but this man, they said, had spent twenty-eight years in Cuba. The girls soon learned that although his name and his features were not Cuban, his speech and his expressions certainly were. The speaker's opening humor claimed the attention of the congregation, but soon he became serious about his purpose for being there. Maria felt she had learned much about the teachings of Holy Scripture at Santa Margarita High School and in the Bible class, but this man tied all the knowledge into a package, labeled it faith in Christ, and presented it to them not as a panacea for the world's woes but a prize an individual could claim. With a bright flash of insight, Maria saw her need for a personal Savior. She glanced at Juanita. Her friend, she was sure, had gotten the same message.

At the close of his talk, the evangelist invited everyone who wanted to confirm his faith in Christ to come forward. The request seemed strange to the girls. Maria rose hesitantly. Juanita was already on her feet. Together they dedicated their lives to Christ. The price — and the value — of that decision was yet to be proved.

Maria took her commitment seriously. She was baptized and was soon inviting others to share her joy. Among her first successes was her younger brother. Later her mother accepted the evangelical faith. At length her father, too, made his profession.

When Castro succeeded in ousting Batista on New Year's Day, 1959, Maria was almost too busy to take notice. Her mother had fallen ill and was in need of Maria's almost constant care. Initially, Cuban citizens felt little change in their surroundings. Many were happy that the bloody street fightings were over at last. Supposedly aimed at rebels, the indiscriminant blasts from the government's machine guns often claimed innocent victims as well. If Premier Castro carried out all his promises, the people would surely enjoy the new regime.

But the hoped-for reforms, like Mrs. Rosales' health, seemed frustratingly unattainable. Near the end of 1960 the government, in its seizure of businesses, took control of five houses that Senor Rosales owned. The government salary was nothing like the income he had built up. It could not pay for the medicines his wife required and feed his family, too. Maria and her brother worked as often as they could, but jobs were scarce, as was food. The com-

bination of circumstances was discouraging enough
for a well person, destructive for one who was ill.
But Maria's mother seldom complained. She echoed
her daughter's confident faith and inspired the
healthy members of the family, remaining an example of patient waiting until her death in 1963.

Throughout the long illness, Maria and her family
received encouragement from Raul Garcia, the student pastor who conducted the neighborhood mission. In 1964, after Raul graduated from seminary,
the young minister became Maria's husband.

The Garcias' first pastorate was a pioneer mission
in the sleepy farming village of Tierra Bonita in
Matanzas Province. Government interference, they
soon learned, had reached the rural churches. A
"Law of Associations" required them to register with
the government in order to hold services legally.
The statute also forbade any religious activity outside the church and called for periodic identification
of the members. Raul would not agree to require-
ments that denied his Lord's command to "go and
preach" and that endangered the livelihood of his
congregation. His refusal to register, however, did
not cause immediate repercussions. More than a
year later, shortly after the Garcias' first child, Ra-
mon, was born, they received the first foreboding of
trouble.

Early in 1966 the pastor of a church in nearby
San Pedro was expelled from his pulpit by an order
from the Department of Religious Matters. He had
been arrested twice previously for no apparent rea-

son — except that his church and its two branch congregations in outlying villages were growing. With his arrest, the authorities closed all three churches, confiscated the furnishings, and sealed the doors. So strong was the fervor of the parishioners, however, that the congregation continued to win converts. Every Sunday Raul's congregation was swollen by visiting members of the San Pedro church who climbed into the back of a truck for a bumpy ride to worship.

Persistent appeals for the government to remove the sanctions were finally successful. After ten months, the government agreed to permit the churches to open if another pastor could be found. Raul then accepted the call of the San Pedro congregation to take charge of that church and its two missions in addition to his Tierra Bonita parish. When Raul was called to pastor a church in Havana in 1967, the Garcias were convinced that the people in San Pedro and Tierra Bonita were prepared to carry on.

Maria's home town had changed a lot during their three years' absence. The former resort gaiety of Havana — muffled by the Communist experiment before their departure — had been replaced by an oppressive pall of fear. The Committee for the Defense of the Revolution had tightened its surveillance over the million Havanans. The activities of all citizens and particularly of Christians were closely observed. Words they uttered in public were now chosen carefully. To mention even casually a church

item, or to be caught carrying a Bible, invited arrest.
Jailings were frequent. Raul was taken into custody
repeatedly for questioning. On one occasion he was
measured for a prison uniform, but he was never
jailed. How long he would be spared he did not
know.

In spite of the State's aggressive policy against the
church, Maria and Raul discovered that the people
turned more and more toward God, though defying
the state could be very costly. As the nation's sole
employer, the government was in a position to de-
prive anyone of his means of livelihood, a penalty
that was often imposed for the crime of church membership. Despite the danger of being labeled a
Christian, fourteen persons made a public profession
of faith and were baptized during the Garcias' first
year in Havana. In their second year, twenty dared
to take the step. Membership statistics held little
meaning, however, as evangelism was forced under-
ground and as some church members fled the country. For every public profession of faith, there
would be a number of private professions by people who dared not appear in church; for every new
member added there were many old ones dropped
from the list as they left the country. Victory, however, was not in recorded numbers but in people's
lives.

Christians found their faith becoming stronger under persecution. Those sent to prison carried their
strengthened beliefs with them. Ex-prisoners who
joined Raul's parish told of finding Christ and peace

through the witness of fellow inmates. Courageous parishioners continued to invite others to worship, though risking an unwitting contact with a member of the CDR.

One evening Maria was pleased to see in the congregation a woman who had previously refused all invitations to attend. But the worried look on the lady's face bothered Maria. When the woman began to sob, Maria escorted her to the foyer. "May I ask what's the matter?" she said quietly.

Haltingly, the woman told Maria her story. When her son had been drafted for military service, her daughter-in-law and the children had gone to America. The time came for her son's discharge, but the military refused to release him. He had decided to escape from camp and attempt to leave the country on a raft. He was captured twenty miles from his base in a stolen army truck. The mother got the word about her son's imprisonment just that day and in the afternoon she had received another invitation to visit the church. This time she decided to come. "But what good can you do me?" she finished. "Nothing can save my son. The penalty for desertion is death."

Maria told her about the help God offers his children and the peace that comes with reliance upon his Son. Then she guided the lady back to her pew to listen to Raul's sermon. At the end of the service the troubled woman resolved to give her problem and her life to Christ. As she grew in her faith, she was able to put the fate of her son completely in

the hands of God, serenely trusting him, whatever
the outcome.

While attending to the often distressing needs of
their congregation, the Garcias were facing increasingly difficult problems of their own. Carmen had
been born shortly after their arrival in Havana and
then baby Ernesto joined them. With each of the
three births Maria's health had weakened. The rigid
rationing of goods and the rising cost of medicines
deprived her of a chance to regain strength. Because of the economic plight of his parishioners and
the demands of the government, Raul's income remained frustratingly inadequate. The people gave
as best they could, but it was hardly sufficient. From
Raul's meager salary of sixty pesos a month, eighteen had to be paid to the state as a self-employ-
ment tax.

To get food for his family took time as well as
money. Raul had to replace his practice of morning
Bible study, prayer, and sermon preparation with
a new schedule of rising at four every morning to
stand in lines for his family's daily supply of food.
Not that the rice, bread, and milk that he could af-
ford were ever enough. To keep the children from
suffering too much, the parents deprived themselves.
A thin slice of bread with coffee made up their
breakfast. For lunch they went without bread as
well as meat, sipping a spiceless, meatless soup. For
supper they allowed themselves a little of their individual beef allotment of twelve ounces a week.
Along with their fellow citizens, the Garcias pur-

chased second-class beef, not only because of their
economic squeeze, but because the first-class meat
was either exported or used by elite restaurants or
supermarkets catering to foreign socialists.

Several times a week Maria and Raul would visit
a restaurant and wait sometimes for hours to get
their food. This was not an extravagance for the
Garcias; since there was so little to buy, purchasing
was reduced to a matter of priorities. In a country
where a person could buy only one pair of shoes a
year and hunger had become a way of life, it was
not uncommon to see a number who were barefoot
among the queues of people waiting for food at a
restaurant.

When the Garcias' refrigerator broke down, they
knew it could never be repaired. As with most
mechanical products from the United States, replacement parts were not obtainable. Because the baby's
milk and special medicine for Ernesto, who had de-
veloped digestive trouble, had to be cooled, Raul
found it necessary to go to the Secretary of Public
Health for permission to purchase ice and then stand
in line all morning, every morning, to get it.

As the vexations of daily life bore down upon
the young parents, they faced the urgent question:
Should we, as many others have done, leave our
homeland? For themselves, they were content to
stay despite the hardships of daily living. But they
knew that if they continued to deny themselves necessary sustenance, their own health would eventually
become so impaired that they would not be able to

care for the children they were trying to save.

"Lord," Raul prayed one evening, "we don't know what to do. Should we leave for the children's sake? It gets harder every day to see them suffer. I really cannot serve my congregation the way I ought. Yet I do not want to leave them. Please show us your will."

At the end of the prayer time, Maria said, "Raul, I wonder if we shouldn't apply for permission to leave Cuba. You know how long it takes — months and months, sometimes years — just to get permission to leave. In the meantime — "

"Maria! The same thing occurred to me while we prayed. The Lord must have directed it," Raul broke in, then finished the thought: "In the meantime, we will continue to serve and seek God's will."

"I have another prayer," Maria said and bowed her head. "Lord, if it is your will that we leave Cuba, would you give us a sign? If the permission takes a long time, I will know it is your desire that we stay, and we will withdraw our request. If it takes a short time, then we will leave our country."

Three weeks after the application had been submitted, the Garcias received word that they could leave. Maria was dumfounded. Surely this was God's answer, but still she was reluctant to go. Along with the authorization to leave the country, the government had reminded the Garcias of an important obligation: every able person leaving Cuba had to first join a "volunteer" workcamp for a period of time that fluctuated at the government's whim from a few months to several years. Mercifully for Maria, whose strength had been sapped by the poor diet and constant vigilance over Ernesto, the requirement was waived for mothers of small children. But Raul would have to serve.

Again they entered the valley of decision. After prayer Raul stated flatly, "Here's how we will do it," and outlined his plan: Maria and the children would go to Miami. Raul would go to the workcamp.

"No! I don't want to leave you," Maria voiced her spontaneous objection. But even as she spoke she knew that the course had been unmistakably directed by God himself.

In Miami Maria was to discover a vastly different existence. Although bleak by American standards, her new life would offer a chance to rebuild her strength and give her the joy of seeing her children properly cared for. In their one-room apartment in Miami's "Little Cuba" — bare of all but the essentials, fourth-hand beds, worn table and chairs, and well-used cooking facilities — Maria learned that fellow Cubans took care of their own with little outside help. And she was grateful.

But a part of her would remain in Cuba until authorities there decided her husband's workcamp service had been fulfilled, whenever that might be. Some emigrants, she was told, had spent more than two years in the camp. Until that future, indefinite reunion, Maria's link with Raul and all of her suffering countrymen would be frequent, heartfelt prayer.

*A leap to freedom. Refugees reach U.S. shores after precarious journey in small sailboat.*

Clarence Sallee, *Miami Herald*

*Chapter Three*

# LAW OF THE GUN

"Smile, Carlos," the sinewy Cuban told himself as he approached the ramshackle barracks. "Things could be worse." But he really didn't see how they could be, humanly speaking. Working in mushy sugarcane fields during Cuba's rainy season, plodding along the muddy furrows, and stooping to lay the cuttings in the slough all day, was bad enough, but to come "home" to a pigpen! He hesitated at the entrance, as if to gain the courage to enter. The structure had no walls, merely wire screening stretched around four corner posts that supported a plank roof. It offered very little protection from the steady drizzle, none at all from the occasional hurricane winds. The roof boards were unshingled and widely cracked, inviting a constant dripping over the bunks. Although the beds had been draped with nylon tarpaulins, Carlos knew he faced another uncomfortable night with the insistent raindrops splattering on his head. But what could he do about it? In order to carry out his desire to leave Cuba, he had to put up with it. Better to smile than to cry.

As he entered the pigpen-turned-barracks he slipped on the slime that covered the concrete floor, grabbing a nearby bunk to stop his fall. "Ugh! I wouldn't want to fall in *that!*" a roommate called.

Carlos managed a smile. He looked up at the source of the sludge: a pig lot at the top of an adjacent hill formed a runoff during the long rainy season for the messy stuff oozing across their floor. "The pigs are getting back at us for taking their home," he replied.

The animal enclosure housed fifteen men. They were from a variety of social classes — some were laborers, some professional men. Carlos Alvarado was an educator and pastor. But all had a common goal: to fulfill the degrading workcamp obligation before leaving Cuba. "The final humiliation before renouncing our country," thought Alvarado, "but then, my life had a humble beginning."

Carlos was born to Spanish immigrants struggling to build a new life in a small farming village in Oriente Province. Carlos' father died when he was three, leaving his mother with two preschool children to rear. She went to work on the farms, and so did Carlos and his younger brother as soon as they reached school age. Though Carlos begged to attend, school was not to be a part of his early boyhood. The family's need for food took precedence over their need for an education. Carlos was eleven years old before his desire to attend school was realized; by working afternoons and evenings he was able to get in half a day of school every morning.

His eagerness to learn speeded his advancement. By the time he was fourteen he had completed the fifth grade. But then he was old enough for a man's job, which meant longer hours on the farm, and he had to drop out of school. A few years later, however, through the ministry of a local Protestant pastor, Carlos committed his life to Christ and acquired a determination to finish his schooling. At the age of eighteen he was a man among the children in grade school — but man enough to stick it out. He wanted desperately to learn, to teach — and to serve Christ. He didn't stop his education until he received a doctorate in education from the University of Havana and a theological degree from a seminary in the United States.

His trip to the United States in the 1950s introduced the young educator to an affluent society he'd never dreamed possible. Many enticing opportunities lured him to remain in the United States, but he resisted the temptation and returned to his homeland, establishing a church in Central Cuba.

The new pastor deplored the high rate of illiteracy that shackled his people. Prodded by his own memory of educational deprivation and his desire that the people read the Word of God themselves, he set up reading classes and dispensed literature supplied by Bible societies.

His church and his ministry grew. By 1959 the parent congregation was supporting a dozen mission congregations in outlying villages and effectively employing the Laubach literacy method of "each one teach one." One of Alvarado's prize pupil-teachers became his wife.

In his desire to get Cubans to read — and to read the right things — Carlos traveled the island in a Bible-distribution effort, supported by the American, Canadian, and United Bible Societies. The ambitious educator-pastor's work soon became recognized. When Fidel Castro came into power Alvarado held the chairmanship of a national association of evangelical ministers and a high office in Cuba's independent council of churches.

Alvarado wanted to believe, like most of the other citizens, that Premier Castro would bring the reforms that Cuba long needed. But he was apprehensive. Before the rebels' victory Carlos' Bible distribution journeys had acquainted him with people who supported Castro and others who mistrusted him. Castroites and Batista soldiers in his own churches had raised many disturbing questions in his mind. Why would Batista's government representative in Oriente hold regular meetings with the rebel leader? When Castro was marching through the flat sugarcane country of the central provinces, why was he not fired upon or stopped in the open? What about the report that Castro was receiving supplies from Batista? Was it possible that a bigger drama was unfolding — one in which, for some sinister reason, Batista was playing the role of villain and Castro the role of hero?

Carlos had tried to shrug off his fears. For a while they seemed unfounded. Castro's policies appeared reasonable; they found acceptance not only at home but abroad. The United States and other countries quickly recognized the new regime. The open killings that had terrorized Cubans during Batista's reign ceased.

But then Alvarado learned that a more insidious extermination had replaced the street shootings. People simply "disappeared." Carlos got a glimpse of the atrocity one night when a soldier knocked at his door.

"Pastor Alvarado?"

"Yes."

"Do you know Pedro Munoz?"

The minister hesitated in his reply. Of course, he knew Pedro. The young man was the son of a member of his congregation. Not long ago Pedro's parents had lost touch with him and had requested congregational prayers in his behalf. As a former officer in Batista's Cuban army, the young Munoz was out of favor with the Castro government. Now one of Castro's soldiers was asking about him. Would it be safe to acknowledge an acquaintanceship?

"Won't you come in?" Carlos asked. As the soldier entered, Mrs. Alvarado slipped into the nursery to check on their sleeping daughter.

The soldier smiled. "It's all right. I'm not going to hurt you. I'm all alone." He pulled something out of his shirt pocket. Alvarado recognized it as a

New Testament. He had distributed many like it throughout Cuba. "This belonged to Munoz. He asked me to give it to you."

Alvarado took the Book. It was one he himself had given to Pedro. He looked at the soldier curiously. "Why is Pedro returning it? Where is he?"

The soldier lowered his voice. "He is dead . . ."

Alvarado frowned. Why hadn't Pedro's parents been told? "Why are you telling me this?" he asked.

"Don't be afraid," the soldier repeated his assurance. "Nobody knows I am here. I just wanted to grant a dying man's last request." The soldier started to leave.

Carlos put a hand on his arm. "Tell me what happened."

The soldier stiffened. Then he told his story. "A few weeks ago Munoz and seventeen others were arrested. I do not know what their offenses were. Our orders were to execute them. Our orders were carried out. Before he died Munoz asked me to see that his pastor, Carlos Alvarado, got the book you now hold in your hands." The soldier again turned to the door.

Alvarado looked at the Testament a moment, then whispered, "Gracias." The soldier was gone.

Carlos pondered the implications of the strange visit. Eighteen people had been killed on government orders and no one — not even the next of kin — had been notified.

Not long after the soldier's nighttime revelation

Carlos was introduced to a more sophisticated purge of former Batista officials, the political well-knowns. Trials were held, but only for publicity purposes. Guilt was inexorably established. Alvarado was asked to join priests and other religious leaders as spiritual counselors to the condemned political prisoners.

The first time he went to the prison, Carlos had reason to be fearful. He knew the deposed government and military leaders were resentful and dangerous. One had grabbed a rifle from a guard while being transported to prison and killed two soldiers before he was gunned down in the street. At the prison, one of the condemned men raised new fears about any eleventh-hour ministry. The man, apparently insane, alternately wept and shouted oaths. Attempts to communicate with him proved futile.

Then a Catholic priest asked Alvarado to join him in conversation with a colonel. "Read the story of the robber on the cross," the priest suggested. Carlos opened his Bible to the Gospel account of the thief being crucified with Christ who was promised a place in paradise upon his last-minute confession. The reading ended, Alvarado talked to the officer about the gift of eternal life. "You know what is going to happen," he concluded. "Do you want to accept Christ?"

The man was quiet for a moment before he said, with conviction, "Yes." Carlos clasped his hand and prayed. The prisoner thanked the men and said, "Would you leave me alone for a moment to pray?" While he was praying, a guard called the group outside.

Except for lights from a jeep, the prison yard was dark. The headlights illuminated a flagpole to which the berserk prisoner had been tied. He was struggling against his bonds when an order to fire was given from the darkness behind the jeep. He made a vain effort to climb the pole, then crumpled to the ground as bullets cut him down.

The colonel and two other officers were handcuffed and marched ahead of the jeep to the rear of the prison yard. The headlamps spotlighted a bullet-scarred wall. One by one the condemned men were blindfolded and placed in the spotlight to hear their last earthly sounds, a command to fire and a volley of shots from the darkness. The colonel was the last to die. He refused a blindfold and asked that his hands be freed. He stood upright between the bodies of his fallen companions and looked confidently into the bright lights as he faced his final earthly moment.

For six months Alvarado's routine included visits to condemned men. Then in the summer of 1959 the pastor was told his services were no longer needed. All the potential enemies from the Batista government, apparently, had been disposed of. The executions did not stop, however. Now they were directed at different opponents of the Castro regime, and no one was to be given a chance to offer last-minute help. The new enemies were the anticommunists, including those who were outspoken critics of the Communists who had gained political power and control of the trade union movement under Batista. For Alvarado the puzzle pieces were falling into place. Under Batista, Communism had been introduced and most Cubans opposed it. Most Cubans also opposed Batista's dictatorship. But what if a "liberator" could emerge to overthrow the despotic dictator? And what if that liberator turned out later to be Communist . . . ?

Eventually Castro openly declared his Marxist loyalty. The disappointed populace felt angry and betrayed, but executions, arrests, and threats of imprisonment kept them in submission. Alvarado was frequently interrogated by the police, especially when he was away from his own community on a Bible-distribution campaign. He soon learned that his best weapon was poise. He faced each session confidently and each time was released for want of condemning evidence. At home his wife, who now had a baby boy as well as a daughter to care for, grew concerned. Carlos reminded her, "I am in God's hands. And so are you and the children. To face up to Communism you cannot be afraid. If you show fear, you are lost. If anyone questions you, be very nice but very firm."

In its continuing attack on the church, the government inducted seminarians and young pastors under a conscription of "unproductive persons." They were placed with homosexuals, conscientious objectors, and habitual criminals in "UMAP camps." The acrostic designation represented an innocent sounding title, *Unidad Militar de Ayuda a la Produccion* (Military Unity of Help to Production), but the letters soon became a synonym for slave labor. The camps were more often referred to by the citizens as "concentration camps," a direct reference to the infamous Nazi prison compounds.

The days were long: fourteen hours of farm labor that started at 5:00 A.M. The food allotment was small. Relatives were permitted to bring inductees food supplies on visiting days, but, with the severe rationing of food to civilians, this could be done only at a sacrifice. In the harvest season the prisoners learned to sneak bites of the products they were gathering — unwashed, uncooked sweet potatoes, tomatoes, or sugarcane — to gain strength just to finish the day's work.

Never knowing when their UMAP service might be completed was particularly frustrating to the inductees. There was no specified length of term. Once conscripted, one would stay in the camps as long as the State deemed it advisable. Alvarado used his office in the council of churches to plead for a change of government position regarding pastors and seminarians. He was rebuffed in one conversation by an official who told him, "Pastors are lazy! Why shouldn't they be treated like other good-for-nothing citizens? If they want to engage in an honest profession, they won't have to worry about conscription into UMAP." He had expressed the sentiment of the State; it was useless for Alvarado to argue further. But he could pray. It was only when word of the injustices of UMAP reached outside Cuba and pressure was applied from international humanitarian and religious organizations that Castro relaxed the conscription and released the pastors.

Alvarado knew the invisible Church — the universal body of believers — could never be destroyed, but he wondered how long the organized church in Cuba could withstand the assaults of the Cuban government. As long as the State made frontal attacks, the church staunchly held out; but when she was struck from within, the people's faith began to flag.

Carlos noticed it first on the local level. Communists would profess faith, become baptized, and get into responsible positions in a church before their party membership was discovered. Carlos even met ordained ministers who held membership in the CDR. Ultimately he heard talk of compromise with the State from officials in the council of churches. Alvarado realized that if the council wanted to survive as a politically powerful entity it would have to support the Castro regime, but he preferred to uphold the Church's historic position of uncompromising faith even if it meant the loss of secular influence.

Others stood with him. It proved a dangerous stand. An increasing number of people who had been arrested and interrogated got word to Carlos that a persistent question placed to them was: "What do you know about Carlos Alvarado?" Other council members were likewise investigated. As the intimidations became more frequent the faithful leadership of the council began to dissolve. Many gave up the struggle and left the country. Council members who favored compromise gained control.

Alvarado was disheartened. To cap his dismay, the Bible distribution program was destroyed when the government outlawed the importation of Bibles. This ministry had already been crippled after U.S. President John Kennedy forced the removal of Soviet missiles from Cuba, and the American Bible Society was summarily denied access. Other societies which continued to send limited amounts of literature encountered the same ban in 1968. Frustrated, the Alvarados filed application to leave Cuba.

In the obligatory workcamp, thankful that his wife and children did not have to experience the animal existence, Carlos determined to smile his way through. It proved a difficult assignment, requiring frequent appeals to God during the two months he was to spend in the camp before his release and emigration to Florida. But it provided him with a rewarding ministry to fellow emigrants. Through his cheerful witness to God's help, he was enabled to lead others to faith in Christ, who, Carlos knew, would yet conquer all the foes of his Church.

# Chapter Four

# YOUNG, IDEALISTIC-AND BETRAYED

"Then there's no liberty in Cuba!" the young man shouted at the stern official. Too late Raphael Atienza caught himself. Why hadn't he kept silent? The frown on the face of the chairman of the Committee for the Defense of the Revolution forecast trouble. Raphael prayed God would keep him from saying anything else; he felt as much regret over his lapse of control as he felt fear over the consequences of his act. When would he ever conquer his impatience? As a self-willed young man, he had been unwilling to curb his lust for life; if there was a forbidden path, he traveled it. Now as a Christian preacher he joyfully took the narrow road to eternal life, but he strained to be free of restrictions that hampered his ministry.

Raphael had grudgingly gone to the CDR headquarters to request permission to transfer supplies from one church to another, chafing at the bureaucracy that made such servility necessary. When the conversation ended in a denial of his request, Raphael lost the patience he thought he had mastered over the ever-tightening controls.

Surprisingly, the CDR chairman said nothing after Raphael's outburst, and the youthful pastor quickly excused himself. Outside, his thoughts raced back almost eight years to 1962 when, as a young man just out of his teens, he had much to learn about self-control. Then he was enjoying the elastic moral standards of the new Cuba. The money he was able to get from occasional jobs or beg from his widowed mother was consumed on gambling, liquor, and women. That his mother objected to his prodigality didn't concern him in the least until the day she told him he could no longer stay in her house.

For a while Raphael solicited drinks from his friends and slept on park benches. That was where his uncle found him one morning. "Get cleaned up," he ordered the youth. Raphael opened his eyes. He sat up, embarrassed that his uncle would find him in such a state. "I've gotten you a job," the older man said.

"I don't want a job," Raphael protested.

"You like sleeping on park benches?" his uncle asked. There was a touch of tenderness in the gruff voice. "You can go back home if you have a job. I promised your mother you'd get one." Silently Raphael climbed into his uncle's car. They drove to a factory where oil filters were assembled.

A tall man seemed to be waiting for them. He smiled and shook hands. "This is Raphael?" he asked.

"Yes," the uncle replied. "He's willing to come to work. See what you can do to reform him."

The foreman winked at Raphael, who frowned suspiciously. "We'll get you acquainted with your duties right away," the man said, waving a hand at Raphael's uncle and walking into an assembly room. Raphael followed. "First meet the crew you will be working with." The man made introductions. As he described the job, he explained the pay scale, which tempered the prospect of working for "Smiley," as Raphael had silently dubbed his superior. He could do a little more drinking and dancing with the money.

At noon Raphael sat with his work crew in the dining hall. Most of them bowed their heads before they ate. The youth sighed. "A bunch of goody-goodies," he told himself, wondering if he could stick it out till pay day.

One of the men caught Raphael's expression and explained, "We're mostly Christians. We usually discuss our faith as we eat. We'd like to have you join us."

Raphael tried to look nonchalant. "Okay," he agreed. "I'll join you. But I don't care about religion. So don't talk to me about Jesus. I live my life the way I want to."

"Fine," replied the worker. "But you won't mind if we have our discussion?"

"Sure, go ahead. It won't bother me." Raphael tried to think about what he'd do as soon as he got paid. He suppressed a chuckle as he thought how he would tell his friends about his mealtime experience. Maybe it would be worth a free drink or two.

But it wasn't easy to ignore his table partners. What they were saying was weird, but even stranger was the way they seemed to believe it. One man, making a point about what life meant without God, started talking about his former love of wine and women. "Terrible," he concluded.

"That's bad?" Raphael muttered.

"For a while, everything seems fine without God," the man said, "but then life becomes meaningless. Old thrills lose their enjoyment. Pleasure becomes pain. But with God — well, when we stop seeking our own pleasures and rely on him for everything, he never ceases to make every challenge a blessing."

When Raphael realized he was staring at the speaker, he quickly returned his attention to the food. Emotional fool! he told himself.

As Raphael listened during the mealtime discussions through the weeks that followed, he heard strange words about heaven and hell, about eternal life and Jesus Christ. He found it becoming harder to be indifferent. If it was true that after death one entered either heaven or hell . . .

Raphael eagerly welcomed his weekly pay. With his old friends again, he could laugh about the odd work crew and all he had to put up with to keep his job. But a gnawing question dampened the enjoyment of his pleasureable pursuits: What if his co-workers were right?

One noontime several men were talking spiritedly about an evangelistic meeting they were preparing for. Raphael thought it strange that they could become so excited about a church meeting. One of them impulsively addressed Raphael. "Would you have any interest in going?"

Raphael heard himself saying, "Yeah, I guess I could go." Then he added, "It might be good for a few laughs."

He fully intended to go just for that purpose, but at the meeting he did not laugh. As the speaker talked, the youth wondered how anyone could describe his own skepticism so well. Raphael returned for other meetings in the week-long campaign. His smugness was shaken. He became painfully aware of the wrong he had done his mother. If there was a God, he had gone against his laws in many other ways as well. In the last meeting the speaker concentrated on the love of God that could forgive all wrongs. Raphael had felt guilt; now he felt God's mercy. When the preacher explained that anyone could claim salvation from the punishment of sin by confessing his wrongs and accepting Christ's forgiveness, Raphael could refuse no longer. When the invitation to trust Christ was given, he joined others at the altar. Surrounding him were his fellow workers, and Raphael felt the joy they had been talking about all along.

As Raphael found reconciliation with his mother, he lost many of his old friends. That didn't keep him from trying to tell them about his new life and his desire that they experience it too. He wanted the world to know this good news of God's forgiveness.

When Raphael joined his new friends in witnessing, he discovered his shallowness of knowledge about the Christian way. He began to read the Bible with an intensity that surprised him. Sadly he lamented the years he had wasted in quest of pleasure. Somehow he had to get the training that would make him more effective in reaching others for Christ. His background hardly seemed appropriate, but he applied for admittance to a seminary and, because of the apparent change in his life, was accepted.

As a seminary student Raphael learned what it meant to suffer for his new-found faith. By becoming a Christian, he stepped onto an upward path, but in the eyes of the State he had become the lowest of humans. In addition to creating a country-wide climate of animosity toward religion, the government took particular pains to harass seminarians with the constant threat of conscription. For pastors and seminary students in 1962, this meant induction into the degrading UMAP camps, which were reserved for Cuba's undesirables. Later it became standard practice to induct seminary applicants into three years of military service. Of the sixteen students in Raphael's freshman class, only he and three others escaped UMAP conscription.

Before his graduation in 1966, the anti-religious campaign worsened. Large numbers of professors and pastors were arrested and charged with immoral conduct or illegal activities. Many were jailed. It was an emotional shock to the young seminarian. As the students were drawn together in prayer, the realization came that in spite of what seemed a defeat for the Church, God was still controlling events. He had permitted the evil to Cuba to occur for his own good reasons; someday Raphael would understand why.

As long as he was able, Raphael took his message of God's love to young Cubans at their youth meetings or on the street. By the end of 1964, evangelistic meetings were forbidden by the government. Church activities were curtailed; pastors were required to apply for permission to hold any kind of meeting other than regular worship services. Raphael's student youth ministry was halted. But he had managed to introduce a number of young people to Christ, including Juanita Ortiz, whom he married upon his graduation from seminary.

At their new pastorate in Santa Clara, the Atienzas learned how complete was State control over the lives of the people. It started early. Already in elementary school, pressure was put on the children to join Pioneers, the Communist youth organization that paved the way for membership in the Junior Communists. To make it harder for youngsters to resist, noisy Pioneer street parties were frequently held just outside the church building at the Sunday school hour. As the young people matured, they faced increasing pressure. Their attendance at religious activities was noted and reports were spread that church membership could dash their hopes of attending college.

High-sounding campaigns lured many youths into evil. "Literacy junkets" into the countryside appealed to many young people, and many pregnant girls returned from the tours. Little was accomplished on these tours to raise Cuba's literacy level, but the Communists had dealt an effective blow to Cuba's close-knit family structure which had obstructed the alien takeover.

When conscription was inaugurated for young people, men and women from fifteen to twenty-seven years of age, into military or agricultural service, morality and integrity suffered another blow. Raphael was eligible for the conscription but he again escaped immediate induction. Many of his church youth were inducted. The conscription was particularly hard for the young teen, especially for a girl who would be taken from her home and parental authority to work in agricultural areas for two months every year. A protest by either the inducted youth or the parents meant the cessation of education.

Young adults who were loyal to both country and God were bewildered by the Communist tactics. The Party splashed publicity across the countryside that linked the government's revolutionary program with Christianity. Ubiquitous posters called Christians to revolution. One showed Jesus carrying a machine gun. Some restless youths eagerly joined the crusade. Raphael understood their confusion. He, too, felt a kindred spirit for action; but he warned them that they could not be both Communist and Christian.

The ideological struggle between the contending forces became so intense that Raphael's congregation split apart — just as the Communists had hoped. Some left the church, beguiled by Castro's promises. Those who remained, however, were stronger in their faith. Later, when Castro's aura of heroism faded, many disillusioned followers returned to the church and were received with open arms.

Those who dared to stand for Christ risked their freedom. One youth, warned by the CDR about his "over-zealous" church attendance, refused to curtail his religious activities. Then he was picked up one evening at his home by the militia. His family knew nothing of his whereabouts for a month. They learned about his experience only when he contracted hepatitis and was brought home so his parents could obtain medical assistance. The boy told of long days of farm labor with little to eat — sardines for breakfast, codfish for the other meal of the day — and a muddy river for washing. The hepatitis, although it brought suffering, provided the means for the youth to return to his family. It was

*Cuban escapees wade ashore on coast of Florida after two-day voyage in their twenty-two-foot sailboat.*

Tom Neel, *Miami Herald*

one of many unusual answers to prayer that Raphael witnessed.

Another boy not quite fifteen was forced to go to a military school for six months. There he experienced constant hunger, not only for food — which was too meager to satisfy a teen-ager's appetite — but for spiritual fellowship. His Bible was taken from him when he entered the school. Later, inexplicably, he was called to the director's office and handed his Bible. "You may read this if you wish," the director told him with an air of indifference, "but" — his voice suddenly imperative — "don't let anyone know it."

The injustice of the government's discrimination toward Christian youth gnawed at Raphael's spirit. When his conversation betrayed his restlessness, older pastors counseled him that restraint was better than a jail sentence. But he found it hard to bridle his emotions when his family — Juanita had presented him with two sons during their three years of marriage — was always hungry and when his ministry had to be neglected so he could wait in the bothersome lines to shop. What vexed him most were the restrictions on his movements. He could not carry a Bible openly or even visit a parishioner without the danger of arrest on a proselyting charge. Every meeting other than scheduled services and every interchange with another congregation had to be approved by government authorities. Often the approval would be given only after a two-week wait.

When action did not come on his request to

move some supplies from another church to his,
Raphael went to the local office to find out why. He
was greeted affably by the man in charge. "Pastor
Atienza, you have come to see about your permit,"
the man stated. "First, let us talk about another
matter. I am chairman of our local Committee for
the Defense of the Revolution. I would like to invite
you to become a member."

Raphael looked at him incredulously. Then he
said as politely as he could, "Thank you, but I don't
believe I would care to."

After several rejected invitations, the chairman
ceased to smile. "You know, you should cooperate
with the government. If you do not, the government will not cooperate with you."

"You mean that you would withhold permission
for a simple request to move church supplies . . . just
to make me join the CDR? I'm sorry, but your
threats won't change my mind."

At length the official terminated the conversation
by picking up a form from his desk and scribbling
on it. He handed it to Raphael and said blandly,
"I'm sorry, but the government of Cuba is unable
to grant your request."

That was when Raphael erupted. Impulsively
he shouted the accusation: "Then there's no liberty
in Cuba!"

That night Raphael received a telephone call. He
was to attend a meeting the next morning in the office of the district CDR chairman. There were a
dozen people in the office when Raphael arrived.

The district chairman lost no time in getting to his business. "You have been accused of a treasonous statement," he told the apprehensive pastor.

"What are you talking about?" Raphael countered. "I have never said anything treasonous."

"What was it he told you yesterday?" The chairman addressed the man who had refused Raphael's request the day before.

"He said strong words against our country and falsely accused us of restricting his freedom."

The chairman turned to Raphael. "You cannot make statements against the State."

"It was hardly a treasonous statement." Raphael tried to sound calm. "It was made in the heat of my distress at being refused a simple request."

Raphael stopped his futile defense. It was obvious that the leader was no longer listening.

"I think we ought to set up court right now to consider this," said the official. A "judge" was appointed, one of the men was asked to keep notes, and the "trial" began.

"You are accused of speaking harshly against the State," the appointed judge addressed the defendant. "We have a witness." The man asked the local official to repeat his charge.

The recitation was repeated slowly for the record, after which the witness added: "But that isn't all. Pastor Atienza also refused to cooperate with . . ."

"I was threatened!" Raphael broke in, then fell silent. There was little use objecting at this point.

Their minds were set. He would just have to wait to see what they might do.

"You are guilty of speaking against the State," the judge was saying. "Are you aware that we could — with our evidence — put you in prison?"

Raphael could scarcely believe that, but he said nothing.

"You know the penalty for treason is death? You don't want that to happen, do you?"

Raphael was silent.

"Do you understand? If you don't cooperate, you may lose your life!"

Raphael nodded. That might be a blessing, he thought.

The chairman whispered something to the judge, who told Raphael, "You have a wife and children. We are going to be lenient with you — this time. But you are to speak no more against the State. Because of your sentiments, you will be the object of close observation."

On his way home Raphael decided to leave Cuba as soon as he turned twenty-seven — the conscription-free age. That was only a few months away. But he received his notice of induction one week later!

Had it not been for laggard Cuban bureaucracy, Raphael would have added the humiliations of involuntary military service to his list of grievances. He had completed his pre-induction physical examination, but his all-important twenty-seventh birthday arrived before his call to service.

He still had a long wait for approval of his request to leave the country, then he had to fulfill his workcamp service. But as the new decade of the '70s dawned, Raphael Atienza and his family landed in America, free at last but with his spirit still bound to his captive countrymen.

*Chapter Five*

# MISSIONARIES IN PRISON

The news Herbert Caudill received in a telephone call on an April evening in 1965 was another chapter in the story of a persecuted Church: the pastor of a Baptist congregation in an outlying province had been arrested.

The report was a shock to the American missionaries, even though they had known it was bound to happen. Harassment of churches had woven a tangled pattern since the 1959 "liberation." At first it had been bureaucratic interference, with regulations and restrictions hampering activities. Later it was strategic annoyances — blocked streets keeping churchgoers from driving to churches or noisy Communist rallies disrupting church services. The Southern Baptist work that Caudill directed was not Castro's only target. Some energetic Pentecostalists had already been jailed. Missions with large educational systems — Catholic as well as Protestant — were shaken by the nationalization of all private elementary and secondary schools. Many church buildings were closed and property was confiscated.

After digesting the caller's excited recital of the arrest, the Caudills talked quietly about their adopted Cuba. A lot had happened since Herbert had come in 1929 and Marjorie had joined him a year later. Initially the political picture had been confusing to the young Americans. They weren't used to frequent and sometimes violent changes of government, but their missionary work had never been seriously hampered. Every year until 1959, the gains had been steady, if not always impressive. They had made many close friends among the Cubans and, while their Georgia-bred serenity was not akin to the fiery latin temperament of their neighbors, they had come to look upon Cuba as home. They had raised their three children there. One daughter, wife of fellow-Georgian David Fite, a professor at the seminary, had also adopted Cuba and only recently had presented the Caudills with their third Cuban-born grandson.

Along with most of the Cuban citizenry, the Caudills had welcomed the rise of Fidel Castro, who promised reforms the nation needed badly. Indeed, members of Baptist churches had fought at Castro's side for a free Cuba. His government takeover on January 1, 1959, had barely become history, however, when the new leader's Marxist leanings were made known.

Fortunately, the Caudills had been able to continue their work. But now what? Did the phone call portend ill? They prayed for the safety of the arrested pastor and other Cuban pastors and went to bed. They had put the situation in God's hands and had no trouble getting to sleep. It took a while for the rapping sound to penetrate Herbert's slumber and become a real noise outside of a dream. Awake at last, Herbert called, "Who is it?"

"The security police."

"Who — the police?" Marjorie was awake.

"What do you want?" Herbert asked. The two slipped into robes and slippers. The bedside clock registered 1:05 A.M.

"We're from the Bureau of Investigation," the voice outside the door announced.

Herbert opened the door to four men. They were accompanied by a distressed woman — the administrator of the seminary — and a student. As the men opened cabinets and pulled drawers in their search of the apartment, the administrator whispered her dismay. The officers had awakened her and made her lead them to the Caudill residence.

The telephone interrupted the hushed conversation. Marjorie went to answer it. Before she could reach the phone, one of the investigators picked it up and curtly dismissed the caller.

A knock on the door was accompanied by a woman's plaintive "Senor Caudill!" Herbert quickly opened the door. "They've taken my father and two other pastors to pris—" Comprehension of the scene shocked her into silence as she witnessed a reenactment of her father's seizure.

The policemen gathered from their search and approached Herbert. In their hands were his diary, several file folders, and his passport. "You are under arrest, Senor Caudill," one of the men said. "You will come with us."

Herbert dressed quietly, breathing a prayer of thanks that his wife was not being taken. He and Marjorie said nothing as the police prepared their separation, yet their eyes carried on a silent dialogue. Mutual assurances of prayer and thoughts of their thirty-five years of marriage — almost all of them spent in the country that seemed now to turn against them — found expression in their fleeting glances.

Three of the policemen led Herbert away and ordered the visitors to go home. One of the intruders stayed behind, determined to pry open a safety box. Marjorie explained that the safe had been given to them and they had never used it. "I'd gladly give you the combination, but I don't know it," she explained. Each of Mrs. Caudill's assurances that the box was empty only renewed the man's exertions to open it.

Marjorie closed her argument with a shrug and sat down to watch the man labor. As the minutes grew into hours, she became fascinated by the box's resistance and wondered if perhaps it contained some secret after all. It was nearly five in the morning when the policeman sighed in triumph as the lid popped off. His victory, however, was as empty as the box.

At last able to go to bed, Marjorie could not sleep. Should she call her daughter? No, she decided. No use getting her upset, or in waking the family. At seven the phone rang.

"Mother!" an anxious voice cried.

"Margaret!" Marjorie responded. "I wondered about calling you . . . we're going to need David's help. They've taken Daddy —"

"I know," her daughter interrupted. "I tried to call you last night. A strange man answered and I knew the same thing was happening to you . . . they've taken David, too!"

In other telephone calls that morning Mrs. Caudill learned that nine of fourteen seminary professors had been arrested and taken away.

Marjorie dressed to go out. She had to see how the students were doing. She went first to the librarian's apartment. Her knock aroused the librarian and also summoned a cluster of students who had witnessed the arrest and were now asking many questions. Inside the apartment the group huddled in prayer, trying to determine what should be done. With the last "Amen," the group looked at Marjorie. "I think I should go to the Swiss Embassy," she said.

The Swiss ambassador was sympathetic, although he could do little except record the incident and promise legal assistance.

A solitary cell awaited Herbert. It was to be his home for eight days. His lonely routine of pacing the floor and praying for guidance was interrupted only for meals and interrogation. The investigative sessions seemed to be filled more with shouted accusations than with searching questions. Caudill was called an agent of the United States' Central Intelligence Agency, and worse, the leader of a spy ring. He was accused of smuggling people and money out of the country and was told the Cuban government had sufficient evidence to convict him.

On the Tuesday following his Thursday morning arrest, Herbert was reunited briefly with his wife. Marjorie and their daughter Margaret, with the Fites' three children — James, eight; John, six; and month-old Mark — met him in a small room. Conversation was conducted cautiously in the presence of a guard. The ten-minute period passed all too quickly. Both the prisoner and his visitors were as concerned about the feelings of the other as they were about the consequences of a misstatement. Herbert said nothing about his frequent interrogations.

When their time together was nearly over, Herbert said casually, "Well, I've seen my wife and daughter and three grandsons. The only one I haven't seen is my son-in-law."

It was the guard who supplied the answer to the unspoken question. "He's here with you."

It was a month before Herbert and David faced trial. Weekly ten-minute visits from Marjorie and the Fites provided a welcome change from the interrogations, making the wait bearable.

After eight days of solitary confinement, Caudill was placed in a four-bed cell with five fellow prisoners — three Cuban pastors, a convicted murderer, and a political prisoner. Because of his advanced age, Herbert was given the bottom bunk. Two men slept on the floor.

Although religious activity of any kind was forbidden, Christian fellowship in the crowded cell could not be stifled. The pastors had been refused Bibles, but someone found a pencil and wrote down Scripture passages on a scrap of paper to use in clandestine "prayer meetings."

The whispered words of encouragement and prayers of the pastors made an impression on the non-Christian occupants. The political prisoner was initially callous toward his "religious" cellmates — he hissed the phrase contemptuously — but he couldn't ignore their curiously optimistic attitude. Just as he seemed open to spiritual help, they were moved to a large cell block of La Cabana Fortress. Four days later their trial came up.

May 14, 1965, was a long day for Herbert Caudill. He felt his sixty-one years in bones that ached from seemingly interminable sitting and listening to false testimony. There was little comfort in the knowledge that his son-in-law and forty-one fellow Cuban pastors and missionaries were suffering the same pains. In a public show of careful deliberation, the prosecution took from eight o'clock in the morning until ten at night to establish the predetermined guilt of the defendants. When charged with teachings that were not in accord with Communist doctrine, Caudill simply stated that he had been teaching the same thing for the previous thirty-six years. He truthfully — but futilely — denied any connection with the United States' Central Intelligence Agency.

The judges ruled as he knew all along they would, rendering a verdict of guilt for "conspiracy against the security and integrity of the State." As "spies," a thirty-year sentence was asked for Caudill; Fite faced an eighteen-year imprisonment. Because of Caudill's age and Fite's family situation, allegedly, the sentences were reduced to ten years for Caudill and six for Fite.

As he was being taken back to La Cabana, Herbert longed to be able to talk with Marjorie. He knew she had been at the trial and had been praying right along for him, though he had been forbidden to look around the room. Once he had heard a baby cry and almost chuckled at this contact with his family: he recognized his grandson Mark's wail. But now there was no one to share the weight of the moment. No one except God.

"Lord," he prayed, "give me a word for this time." The promise of Psalm 46:10 came to him then. He had recited it often in his ministry to comfort others. The verse had always been meaningful, but it was to take on special meaning as the days plodded by:

"Be still, and know that I am God: I will be exalted among the heathen, I will be exalted in the earth."

Caudill's home for the next eighteen months was the Cabana Fortress, an old army barracks converted

into a jail to house the accumulation of prisoners
since the advent of the Castro regime. The com-
pound included a number of sleeping units built
originally to hold thirty-five men each. As prison
blocks, each unit contained two hundred men. Two
lavatories inadequately served each block. Brief
showers were permitted two or three times a week
at the community bath in the open patio connect-
ing the cell blocks — fifty-six showerheads for up
to eight hundred prisoners at a time. Five-minute
meal periods featured a heavy starch diet. The
limited offering of meat was usually tripe or pigs
feet.

The hopelessness of the longtime prisoners —
some jailed at Castro's takeover — was debilitating.
The situation obviously did not inspire optimism,
yet Herbert was able to pick out the Christians
whenever he was shifted, as the prisoners frequently
were, from block to block. They held a hope that
defied their miserable conditions.

At home Marjorie felt keenly what she considered
a divine charge, since her husband was no longer
able to be spiritual adviser of the Western Cuba
Baptist work. She wrote to all of the wives whose
husbands had been imprisoned, assuring them of
her concern and her prayers. Their responses raised
her own spirits. She sensed a grim determination
among the Cuban Baptists to keep going and to be
faithful during this period of testing.

For some it was a grueling trial. The husband of
one close friend, an early Castro prisoner, had been

*Marjorie and Herbert Caudill land in Mexico on first leg of journey back to the United States after arrest and imprisonment in Cuba. Behind Caudills are their daughter Margaret Fite and her husband David with son Mark.*

arrested as he was rocking his two-year old son. Although years had passed since the child witnessed his father forcibly taken from home, the trauma had caused emotional scars he still carried.

Marjorie shared the Cubans' common suffering. She was one with them as she stood in long lines at stores and shops, hoping that when she finally got to the head of the queue the item she sought would not be gone. By frugally rationing her own meager allowances she tried to stock up on staples so that she could supplement Herbert's prison issue in her monthly visits. She added prayer to her shopping list each time she attempted to get scarce clothing items, scarcer meat products, or ingredients for pound cake. The latter was good because it would keep, but hard to accomplish because the ration book allowed only an ounce and a half of flour a month. Several of her friends insisted she take their entire flour allotment so she could make the cake.

On her trips to La Cabana, Marjorie found she was able to comfort others waiting to pay a visit. She got acquainted with a Catholic lady who, despondent at her husband's thirty-year sentence, marveled at Marjorie's ability to smile. "I know I couldn't take it," Marjorie confided, "if I didn't have faith in God."

"I have faith," the woman replied, "but . . ." The magnitude of the situation overwhelmed her — seeing her husband only once a month, and then being separated by two wire fences a foot and a half apart. Later she told Marjorie, "I'm so glad my husband is in the same cell block as yours. You both give us strength." Through such glimpses Marjorie was able to see the prison ministry of her husband and son-in-law.

One day a man stopped at her apartment and introduced himself as a former La Cabana prisoner. "I wanted you to know how much your husband and son-in-law meant to me," he said. He told her he had spent a lot of time in the same cell block with David and became a Christian there. "I tell you the truth," he said, "the only people in that cell block who can take it are the Christians. The rest of us were desperate. Some men went completely crazy."

In prison Herbert sensed that he had a greater opportunity to witness for Christ than he ever had on the outside. He was forbidden to preach, but private conversations could not be closely controlled. Many of the inmates were hardened and bitter men, yet Caudill was able to see changes wrought as God worked in them. One man had not been released when he completed his sentence. He was retained on continuing trumped-up charges. After he had believed the gospel learned in conversations with Caudill and the Cuban pastors, he was able to accept as well his prolonged imprisonment. An imprisoned lawyer — a high Mason, influential in civic affairs in his province — became a Christian while in prison with Caudill and read through the entire Bible.

Although not permitted to bring Bibles, prisoners passed around a few copies brought in previously. Along with a number of English literature books and several Russian books that had been translated into Spanish, Herbert was able to read regularly from the Scriptures. This was particularly helpful during a three-month summer period when visits and mail were cut off. As fall of 1966 approached, Herbert found it increasingly difficult to read. At first he tried to ignore the dimmed vision, telling himself that it was the constant haze caused by the cell block's cigarette smoke. Occasional bursts of brightness in his eyes and a rainbow effect around windows and lightbulbs increased his concern, however.

One day in the bath a Cuban Christian from another block revealed that he was going to be allowed a visit from his family. During the conversation the man asked Herbert why he was squinting. "I've been having a little trouble with my eyes," Herbert explained, describing the condition. Caudill didn't realize at the time that the chance encounter was to be the first link in a chain of events that would eventually lead to freedom.

When word reached Marjorie through several repetitions of the conversation that the Cuban friend had with his family, she feared the worst. On a trip to the United States in 1964 Herbert had undergone surgery for a detached retina and finally had lost sight in his left eye. Determined to get help for her husband, she went to the authorities with

the story. They were sympathetic to her earnest plea
and promised to do something. Prison officials arranged to have Herbert go twice to a local Havana
hospital for eye examinations. He later spent four
days in the military hospital where he was examined with extra care. Each time he was returned to
La Cabana.

*Caudills, at right, and Fites at televised press
conference in Atlanta, Georgia, after their
release from Cuba.*

Baptist Press photo

On November 25, 1966, Caudill was called from the block, taken to a warehouse, and told to take off his prison uniform. In his civilian clothes, he was ordered to a car which drove him to the office of the Bureau of Investigation. After a twenty-minute wait he was called into another office. His wife and the treasurer of the Cuban Baptist Convention were waiting there to take him home.

Caudill signed "provisional liberty" papers and was told he was being released "so you will be able to see an eye doctor." He was cautioned that his movements were restricted to the immediate area of his apartment in Havana. He was not to attend any political or social gatherings, which ruled out participation in worship services. Word passed quickly, however, that Senor Caudill was home. The first night of his return, rejoicing well-wishers almost got him into trouble. A few came from one church and several from another until more than twenty people had assembled for an impromptu, forbidden gathering in the Caudill apartment.

The following March two eye specialists, Dr. William S. Hagler of Atlanta's Emory University, and Dr. Harry Taylor of Norfolk, Virginia, went to Cuba to perform a retinal operation on Herbert's eye. The Americans, who performed the surgery in a public operation in a hospital in Havana, left behind $2,000 worth of equipment.

A few weeks earlier David's parents, Mr. and Mrs. Clifton Fite of Waynesboro, Georgia, had traveled to Cuba in an apparently unsuccessful plea for the release of their son. Nothing happened until November of 1968 when twelve-year-old James was permitted to leave the country on a flight to Mexico. He flew from there to his grandparents in Waynesboro.

By this time Marjorie's eyes were giving her trouble. The poor diet and the tensions of life in Castro's Cuba were taking their toll. Efforts were increased to secure David's release so that the whole family might be able to leave Cuba.

In December, quite unexpectedly, Cuban authorities released David from prison. The Fites and the Caudills applied for permission to leave the country and were on a flight to Mexico in February, 1969. The veteran missionaries, with turbulent feelings, left the country that for nearly forty years they had called home.

*Chapter Six*

# PIONEERS FOR SLAVERY

Lolita Valdez was only eighteen months old when Fidel Castro was named Cuba's premier. While the evolution of Cuba's Marxist government claimed little of Lolita's attention, her development was of vital interest to the State. The government took firm control of the education of Cuba's youth, and Lolita's parents felt a sharpened responsibility for their daughter.

In their family prayers, Bible reading, and regular Sunday morning worship, Lolita's parents strove to foster her spiritual growth. As a skilled craftsman in Havana, Senor Valdez was able to provide his family with material comforts until the economy was "customized" by Castro. A large television set, purchased on Lolita's first birthday, symbolized the family's membership in Cuba's eroding upper-middle-class society.

Because she had always enjoyed Sunday school, Lolita could hardly understand her parents' anxiety about sending her to kindergarten at the public school. She was vaguely aware of governmental intrusion in raucus Communist rallies outside the church on Sunday mornings and the increasing difficulty of obtaining rationed necessities, but she had yet to experience Communist indoctrination.

From conversations with other parents, Lolita's mother and father knew the dangers besieging a child in public school. Friends had told them of the evil duplicity of one teacher with their kindergartner. The teacher asked her pupils to close their eyes tightly and pray to God to give them ice cream. When they opened their eyes and found no ice cream, she had told them that God, like all fairy-tale characters, could not answer their prayers. Then she asked them to close their eyes again and pray to Premier Castro for ice cream. As they did so, the teacher quietly placed ice cream cups on their desks. When they opened their eyes and giggled in delight, she said, "You see who can answer your prayers!"

Some parents, fearful of losing their children to Communism, had tried keeping them at home. But in such cases the mothers were often sent to work-camps for three months and the children became virtual wards of the State their parents had hoped to isolate them from. Other parents whose teen-age children had been subjected to several years of Communist education lived in fear that an antigovernment expression might be overheard by their own offspring and reported to authorities.

There were, Lolita's parents knew, a few non-Communist teachers in the public schools. But their number decreased every year as graduates from government training schools replaced them. Christian high-schoolers, hopeful of obtaining teaching certificates or entering other professions, were systematically culled out. Application questionnaires asked, in addition to academic queries, whether the applicant believed in God or attended church. The ones who answered affirmatively were never included in the roster of those accepted for higher education.

Ultimately, the Valdezes had little choice but to send Lolita to school and hope for the best. They tried to prepare her for the possible indoctrination by frequent devotional periods centered around the Christian's loyalty to God, not knowing how severely their daughter's loyalty would be tested.

Lolita had learned the basic philosophy of right and wrong — epitomized by God and the devil — at Sunday school. In kindergarten she was introduced to a new teaching about good and evil — this time characterized by the glories of Premier Castro and the villainy of the United States. The indoctrination was at times as subliminal as the constant repetition of Castro's name. A basic arithmetic problem might be phrased: "If Senor Castro has two pencils and gives you one, how many will he have?" At other times, it was less disguised. The class often heard the story of how Premier Castro battled bravely to free Cuba from the Batista dictatorship and boldly rescued Cuba's sugarcane farms and businesses from piggish Americans. The stories never told, of course, how the nationalization of industry and the hostility toward America had sealed off capital and prompted sanctions that seriously affected Cuba's economy, resulting in the tight rationing, of playthings as well as necessities, that had cramped the kindergartners' lives as long as they could remember.

It wasn't until Lolita entered first grade, however, that she felt the sting of religious persecution and the loneliness of being a Christian in a Cuban school. "This is an important year for you," the teacher enthused early in the session. "This is the year you join the Pioneers." She outlined the fun ahead for the members and told them that everyone was expected at the first meeting the following day.

At home that evening, when Lolita mentioned that she would be late coming home the next day because the class would hold a Pioneer meeting, her parents trembled. As carefully as they could they explained that the Pioneer Club was a training ground for the Junior Communists. "The Communists don't believe in God, Lolita. You should not join the Pioneers."

"Teacher didn't tell us that," Lolita objected. "She told us about all the parties we'd have and the projects we could do and the games we'd play."

Senora Valdez pulled her small daughter into her arms, wondering how she could tell a first-grader that these were not the important things of life. "Did your teacher tell you that you have to salute the Communist flag and say a Communist pledge?" she asked. "These things go against God . . ."

"No. Teacher just told us about the fun. She didn't say anything about a pledge, but she said we were all supposed to come."

"Lolita," her father broke in, "we know people whose children have joined the Pioneers. They thought they could join and still be Christians. Once they got in and found out they had to turn away from Jesus, they were sorry, but they found it wasn't easy to get out."

Lolita was perplexed. Obeying the teacher meant making her parents unhappy. But to follow her parents' wishes would be to disobey her teacher, something she had never done. "I don't want to hurt Jesus," she said at last, "but what should I tell Teacher?"

"I guess you will just have to tell her that your parents won't let you join."

At the close of school the next day, Lolita found that breaking the news to her teacher was not easy. She was heartened that other children had come with the same message, but this comfort was dispelled when the teacher jotted down each name and told the dissenters, "Your parents will have to be reported for this."

In the morning the teacher asked that every student stand and share what he had enjoyed at Pioneers. Lolita flushed as she stood to tell the group that she was one who had not joined them. As the scene was repeated each week, Lolita noticed that the number of nonmembers was dwindling.

There were times when Lolita, too, felt it would be easier to go against her parents' wishes and attend the meetings. Between the weekly ordeal of turning down overtures to join the Pioneers, nonmembers were subjected to continuing ridicule because of their decision. Though she tried to please the teacher, Lolita's work never seemed to be satisfactory. Nor did any other nonmembers', including that of Lolita's friend Anne, an advanced pupil who recited well whenever she was given the opportunity. The teacher, nevertheless, was able to find something wrong with every answer. The disdain of the teacher was reflected in the subsequent taunts the Pioneers directed toward nonmembers.

Lolita and Anne shared their loneliness, spending almost every recess together, avoiding the other children. If they weren't together at recess it was usually because the teacher was keeping them in. The reason was invariably for "poor classwork," but the time was often spent in recruiting for the coveted 100 percent membership in the Communist organization. She might entice them with glowing descriptions of the fun the girls were missing — not only games and projects at every meeting but special parties, usually held, the girls knew, during the Sunday school hour. Intimations that grades would improve with joining and appeals to make the teacher's record look better were persuasive. In desperation at the girls' obdurance, the teacher suggested, "You could stay for just one meeting without telling your parents — until you got home and told them how much fun you had."

She was dangling a tempting morsel before the first-grade girls. They wanted very much to please their teacher — and yet do their parents' bidding. They were silent for a moment. Finally Anne replied, "No, I love God and you tell lies about him in Pioneers. Mama says I cannot join, and so I cannot join. I'm sorry if it makes you look bad." Lolita looked wide-eyed at her friend for a second, then stared at the floor. She was afraid to look at the teacher, who was struggling for words. "How about you, Lolita?" she managed at last. Unable to speak, Lolita slowly shook her downcast head. Providentially, the recess period ended before the conversation could be continued.

Lolita admired her friend's bravery, but — although she joined Anne in proudly proclaiming herself a Christian to her classmates — she knew she could never equal Anne's boldness toward her teacher. After the small girl's strong testimony, her teacher found new occasions to ridicule. "How's our little *Christian* doing in her mathematics today?" she might ask amid the laughter of the classroom. Lolita continued her close association with Anne, suffering every ridicule with her.

Second grade provided a merciful respite for the girls. Their new teacher claimed to be neither Christian nor Communist, but the Christian students soon learned that they had a benefactor in her and crowded around her at recesses. Because she had to do it, she gave the children an opportunity to join the Pioneers, but if her class was far below the desirable percentage of membership, she showed little concern. She often brought cookies and milk to supplement the diet of the many youngsters whose parents were financial victims of the nation's depressed economy.

The students were too young to understand what the consequences of the teacher's actions might be, but they appreciated her respect for their beliefs. It wasn't until Lolita came to the United States several years later that she learned what her teacher's stand had cost. In a letter to Lolita, being careful not to place any blame on the government, she wrote that she was staying with her brother since her husband had been in "concentration." The responsibility for their considerable amount of property had been taken over by the generous government. She was no longer teaching. She didn't have to say why she had lost her job.

In the summer between Lolita's second and third grades, she discovered the deep resentment of many Cubans against the Communist regime. As with most citizens, her parents were routinely cautious about their speech. Little was ever spoken about the government in private conversation. Of course, consternation at the long wait for making every purchase and frequent frustration at not being able to get the desired items after the interminable waiting was not always masked. Lolita's Aunt Aida was one who could not easily hide her feelings, though the retribution of the Communist government had reached her husband early in the Castro reign. Uncle Alberto had been in jail as long as Lolita could remember; but, then, so many of the girl's acquaintances had relatives in prison that this seemed as much a part of Cuban life as the waiting in line. It was while standing in an extremely long line that Aunt Aida's repressed emotions surfaced.

Aida had invited Lolita to join her and five-year-old Marita on a trip to Grandmother's. She brought along a large supply of food, not for the train ride, which would be brief, but for the long wait in the ticket line. In better times the trip could have been made by car, but gas rationing, coupled with the difficulty of obtaining American-made automotive parts, had spelled the end of pleasure trips by auto and introduced the incredibly overcrowded train schedule. To get a seat on a train out of Havana in any direction meant waiting for many hours, sometimes days.

Lolita had been able to amuse her younger cousin as they waited through the warm morning, but the oppressively hot afternoon made her wish for a place to get out of the sun. Lolita began to wonder if she should not have come along. At home she could have found shade without worrying about losing her place in the despised line. Why did it have to be so hard just to pay Grandma a visit?

"Lolita." Her aunt's voice broke into her thoughts. "Would you see if you can find a newspaper? I need something to put over Marita's head.

I think the sun is making her sick." Lolita looked at her cousin. Marita's languid eyes were glazed.

"You shouldn't teach her to be afraid of the sun," chided a young soldier who had been standing behind them. "She will have to learn to be in it all day. Soon it will be her privilege to pick tomatoes for her fatherland." He was referring, Lolita knew, to Premier Castro's annual call for the citizenry to work in the harvest fields to abate the chronic food shortage.

Lolita's aunt was able to control her anger only a moment before she exploded. "You live on slogans, don't you!" Waving her arm at a *"Patria o Muerte"* poster on the station wall, she exclaimed, " 'Fatherland or death' indeed! You'd have my daughter die of the heat so she could pick tomatoes for our 'Fatherland'! And who would eat the nice red tomatoes? The Russians! While we'd be lucky to get the culls. Before my little daughter has to pick up one tomato in our 'Fatherland's' farms, she'll be in the United States!"

Lolita was certain her aunt could not have said a worse thing. The surprised soldier, however, backed away from the unexpected onslaught. When he saw that all the other people in the queue were obviously sympathetic to the lady who had dared to speak her mind, he said no more.

A month later Lolita entered the third grade, full of eight-year-old optimism, the incident at the train station forgotten. Her teacher, a harsh young women just graduated from the government training school, soon dampened her enthusiasm, however. "I will be your mother while you are in school," she explained on the first day. And indeed much more of the children's waking hours would be spent in the classroom than at home, for the school day had been lengthened. The children would be under the control of the school from 8:30 in the morning until 5:30 in the evening. The additional hours of school-time wearied the youngsters — and their teacher. She screamed at their late-afternoon mistakes, directing her most vehement sarcasm toward those who refused to affiliate with the Pioneers.

It all seemed very unfair to Lolita. At home and at Sunday school it seemed reasonable to accept all she had been told about God, but at school she was one of only a few who professed such faith. The children who joined the Pioneers or recited Communist teachings in class were the ones who made the good grades and had all the fun. Maybe her parents were wrong. Where was God when she prayed for better days at school? Perhaps, after all, he was like the fairies — useless, unreal.

"Why do I have to go to school?" she asked her mother at bedtime one evening. "As long as I'm known as a Christian I'll never make good grades. The teacher doesn't like me; the other kids tease me."

"Don't you have any friends at all?" her mother replied.

"Just Anne."

"And One other? Have you asked Jesus to help you?"

"Yes, lots of times. But it doesn't do any good. The kids still tease, and I still don't please the teacher."

Her mother hesitated in her reply, grasping for the right words, praying for wisdom. "Have you asked him to . . . just be with you? And to help you live for him in spite of what others do to you?"

Lolita reflected. She really hadn't prayed that way. *Could* he make it all right? She wanted to believe that she could face another day at school, but she knew from experience what would probably happen.

"Will you give him another chance?" Lolita's mother asked. Lolita nodded and fell into wearied sleep.

She thought the next day went a little better. It wasn't any easier to listen to the teacher's ridicule or to the other children echoing her, but knowing she was pleasing Jesus seemed to help.

Before long the Christmas season arrived, bringing its annual spate of good cheer that even a Communist teacher couldn't dispel. For Lolita the season took on added meaning that year. Her father had made application for his family to leave Cuba. As in everything else, there would be a long wait to receive the permission, but the decision had been made and the first step had been taken.

Thoughts of the future, however, had to take second place in the mind of a third-grader who was dreaming about Christmas gifts. Lolita would later recall with dismay the request she made, but she had no idea what the acquisition of her desire would entail. When she heard the announcement that a large Havana department store had a supply of Christmas items and saw a beautiful record player on television, she begged her father to get her one.

"All right," he promised, "I will make the line for you." He hoped it might help his daughter forget some of her unhappiness.

He arrived at the store early in the morning, but a long line had already formed. The television announcement had apparently attracted many. Only a few at a time were admitted into the store. Lolita's father was in sight of the door when he felt he could take it no longer — he gave up and arrived home at 2 A.M. Lolita's mother went that afternoon to stand in the line, returning at five the next morning empty-handed. Aunt Aida then took a turn in the line until noon, when Senor Valdez resumed his vigil. This time he made it into the store, only to learn that the day's quota of record players had been sold.

When Lolita awoke on Twelfthday — the traditional January 6 Epiphany gift day in Cuba — she was greatly surprised to find a record player with her name on it among the gifts. Another aunt, who had been able to get a phonograph of her own, had learned of Lolita's request and had made the gift possible. After three more days of line jockeying,

Lolita's father obtained a replacement for his sister.

Lolita knew the record player had been acquired through the special efforts of her father, mother, and aunt, but it wasn't until the family's permission to leave Cuba was received in July that she realized how great their sacrifice had been. Lolita had offered to help pack for the trip to America. "There won't be much to pack, I'm afraid," her mother told her, explaining that they weren't allowed to take anything with them except a change of clothes.

"What will happen to all of our things?" the little girl asked.

"They will go to the Cuban government."

"Everything? Even my record player?"

Her mother nodded.

When the Valdez family left their house for the last time, police locked and sealed the doors and windows. Everything that Lolita had associated with home was now irretrievable. After tearful goodbyes, the Valdezes took the somber ride to the *Laguito*. The emigration center was a frightening chamber of horrors for a Cuban child departing the country. Lolita reached for her father's hand as they entered the gray building. Inside, the dingy rooms and halls were lined with people, individuals or family groups waiting, ever waiting, for their final taste of Cuban bureaucracy. Many of the expatriates were sleeping, stretched out on the floors, the *Laguito* their only home now that their own had been shut and sealed.

The *Laguito* proved the epitome of inefficiency,

almost as if the uprooting was planned to be grindingly frustrating. There were papers to be approved, new forms to be filled out, inoculations to be received. And in between each process the endless waiting. Perhaps most grating to the emigrants was the air of suspicion that surrounded the examinations. Even children were stripped and examined to ensure that no contraband was being smuggled out of Cuba.

As the process dragged on, Lolita wondered if something would yet detain them. "What happens if they don't let us go, Mama?" she whispered. "We can't go home. They sealed it up."

"I'm sure Aunt Aida will let us stay with her," her mother answered. "I understand that many people have to wait a couple of days before they get to leave." What she didn't tell her daughter was that a simple technicality might prevent their departure. Some, she knew, had been denied embarkation for an unpaid phone bill.

At the end of the exhausting day, the Valdezes, as Mother predicted, found lodging for the night with Aunt Aida. The next day brought more of the paperwork, the dreaded inoculations, the humiliating stripping and searching, the waiting. And at the end of the day another night at Aunt Aida's.

It wasn't until their third visit to the *Laguito* that the Valdez family satisfied the Cuban authorities. They were allowed at last to make their flight to freedom, and the Communist brainwashers were denied possession of one young life.

*Desperate effort to flee Castro's Cuba avoids
disaster through watchful eye of U.S. Coast
Guard.*

7th U.S. Coast Guard District official photo

*Chapter Seven*

# VOICE OF HOPE

What had gone wrong? Domingo Fernandez wondered. Along with most Cubans, the popular radio minister had looked expectantly to the Castro coup as the beginning of a democratic society. But why were the Communists, who had gotten a toehold in the government under Batista, being so obviously favored five months later? If they were allowed to gain power, Fernandez was certain, the revolution would be for nought. He didn't like it.

When he expressed his apprehensions to others, he encountered a surprisingly negative reaction. Fellow pastors, wanting desperately to see the new government produce its promised reforms, suggested that Fernandez ought not to jump to conclusions until the new administration had had a chance to prove itself.

Fernandez insisted that the church should not stand idly by and watch Communism take over. To buy time now would only mean a sellout of freedom

later. His Cuban ministry spanned twenty years as
a parish minister, twelve as a seminary professor
and radio preacher. He didn't want to see it all dissolve. But he waited; and as he waited, he watched.

In April 1960 — fifteen months after the Castro
takeover — Fernandez was handed a propitious opportunity to herald a warning against the Marxist
influence of the government. He had been asked to
address a Cuban Baptist Congress. It was a year
prior to Castro's official proclamation that Cuba was
indeed a socialist state, but Fernandez warned the
pastors that Cuban Communism was coming. He
urged them to speak out against the infiltration and
to prepare for the persecution which would surely
follow Communist usurpation.

In Fernandez' audience was a captain in Castro's
army. At the end of the delivery someone warned
Domingo: "If I were you, I would not give such a
counterrevolutionary sermon again. Believe me, it
is a very dangerous course."

Fernandez considered his own danger, but determined not to stop warning the church about the
greater danger of Communism. He prepared a
widely distributed pamphlet urging Cuba's Christians to look into their Bibles that they might not
be led away by deceivers. Shortly after the pamphlet was published, he was visited by a friend in the
government medical service. "Domingo," she
warned, "this is the beginning of the end. You had
better pack your things and be ready to leave. If
you stay, you will surely be arrested and jailed."

"Thank you for your concern," he told her, "but until the Lord indicates that I should leave, I must continue to exhort God's people."

That night Fernandez received the first of many post-midnight telephone calls. Each call included threats and obscenities. Fernandez began to wonder if the next sermon might be his last. He felt a desperate urgency to prepare his listeners for what he knew would be a fiery test of faith. It wasn't long in coming. Early in 1961 all private and religious schools were taken over by the government. This was followed by expulsion of hundreds of foreign and even some Cuban priests. The government's attitude toward religion was abundantly clear.

Strangely enough, it was a link with Fidel Castro himself that spared Fernandez for some time. One of Castro's sisters was a member of his congregation. He was thankful for her intercession, though he did not know how long even this could help. But until God directed otherwise, he felt he must continue to preach against the now obvious Communist threat.

One year after his address at the Baptist congress, Fernandez was warned by a telephone call that he was on a government list of people to be killed. Was it just another harassment, he wondered, or was it part of a new, very real crackdown following the disastrous Bay of Pigs invasion? Whatever the import of the message, subsequent events vindicated his months of admonition and marked a turning point in his Cuban ministry. A few weeks after Castro's forces overwhelmed the would-be liberators at the Bay of Pigs, the exultant premier announced what the world by that time had guessed: Cuba was a member of the Communist bloc. The State take-over of news media spelled the doom of Fernan-dez' radio ministry, but he continued his seminary and local parish work, albeit in the face of increas-ing government restrictions.

Fernandez was forced to ask himself if his work in Cuba was over. Friends, particularly those with contacts in the government, were urging him to leave. They insisted he was in great danger. "Go to the United States," they pled. The prospect was inviting. His two grown children were already liv-ing there with their families. But any indication that he was to leave would have to come unmistakably from God. He did not want to be swayed by the ad-vice of men, however convincing it might be. He remained at his new task of strengthening the Cu-ban Christians, who were daily suffering ever-greater humiliations.

In mid-September a doctor paid him a visit. "I have heard bad news about you from someone in the government," he told Domingo. "You must leave Cuba. Get out just as soon as you can."

"You ask me to give up my whole life?" Fernan-dez responded. He looked around his office lined with theological texts, reference works, and memo-ries acquired during his years of service. "They'll have to force me out."

The doctor looked incredulously at the preacher. "You will see," he said at last and left.

As such visits became more frequent and ominous, Fernandez pondered the possibility that these were God's messengers, answering his daily prayer for guidance. One visitor told him, "I know someone in G-2." Fernandez frowned — the secret police. "He has learned that you are to . . . disappear." Domingo was aware of the mysterious disappearances of people who were considered enemies of the State. None had been heard from again. His guest echoed Domingo's thoughts: "You won't be much good to your congregation dead." But with Gideon-like insistence, Fernandez wanted additional proof that God wanted him to make the move.

Domingo's answer came in the visit of an army lieutenant, a member of the secret service. "You are a marked man," the officer told Fernandez. "I have seen your name on The List. If you do not leave Cuba soon, you will not live to have another chance."

As he sought God's direction for his next step, Domingo remembered the police captain who had been a member of one of his former congregations. He arranged a meeting. "I've come to you for advice," he told the captain. "You are no doubt aware of the threats on my life. I want you to tell me as a friend exactly what I should do. I believe your answer will come from God."

"God has indeed given you wisdom," the captain replied. "I received word about you only this morning . . . as your friend, I beg you to leave the country before the tenth of October."

Fernandez blinked. Had he waited too long? October 10 was only two weeks away.

"Lord," he prayed with his wife that evening, "if it is your will that I leave, you will have to open the way. I don't see how I can do it before my execution date." Accomplishing anything in Cuba that required government approval had come to mean a long drawn-out process. And how could a marked man effect an escape?

Then Domingo had another visitor. The secretary of the American Baptists in Cuba called on him. "It is very dangerous for you to stay in Cuba," he said.

Domingo smiled. "So I've come to understand."

"I think I can get you out — if you could leave at a moment's notice."

"What about my wife?"

"She would have to stay, but her life is not in danger. You have been the outspoken one. We will see that she follows later."

"How are you going to get me out?"

"I am on a committee of the World Council of Churches that is arranging flights out of Cuba for priests and Protestant pastors no longer welcome here."

"But my denomination is not a member of the council."

"I know it, but I am going to see if I can get you on a flight. The American Baptists are allowed four seats on the airplane. I will see that you get one of them. Just get yourself ready to go. Then wait for word from me."

The word came on October 10.

The following January, Domingo's wife joined him in Miami, where Fernandez was helping in a Baptist work among Cuban refugees. As the number of persons arriving from Cuba swelled the community, Domingo's work grew into an independent ministry.

In 1963 he started a radio broadcast directed to Cubans in Miami. Trans World Radio heard of his work and asked him to become a preacher on their powerful station at Bonaire, Netherlands Antilles. Recorded in Miami, the program is broadcast to a vast Spanish-speaking audience stretching far beyond Cuba, which is just one of many areas reached by Domingo Fernandez' voice.

Refugees regularly bring him word of the comfort the broadcast offers to persons listening furtively in prisons and concentration camps as well as in Cuban homes. Through the refugees, Fernandez has also learned of deteriorating conditions in Cuba — and of the bold witness of Christians there. He was told of one prisoner who refused to stop bowing his head for a table blessing when commanded not to pray, even though the disobedience landed him in solitary confinement.

A pastor friend of his, Domingo learned, had spent three years in prison. Not long after his release, he was arrested again for "proselyting" when he was seen holding a Bible in public. The Bible was examined by the investigating officer, who wanted to know about all the names written in it.

"Those are the people I met in prison whom I talked to about Christ. I pray regularly for them," was the pastor's reply.

"This is a violation of regulations," the officer shouted. "You cannot — "

"Will you please read to me the constitution of our country," the pastor interrupted calmly, "and show me where it says I cannot do this?"

"We don't have to read you the constitution!" the officer screamed. "We are the law! You will do what we say."

The pastor knew he was on legal ground, but his land was ruled by outlaws. He was taken back to prison.

Another pastor imprisoned with equal lack of condemning evidence began immediately to talk to fellow prisoners about his reliance on Christ. "Be quiet!" an inmate shushed him. "Do you want to get yourself killed and the rest of us in deep trouble?"

"No, I just want to get you out of deeper trouble," he replied.

"But we don't want the lieutenant to hear you. He's a mean one."

Some of the men, however, were anxious to hear the comforting words of the new prisoner. A lookout was posted to watch for the lieutenant.

But somehow the prison officer heard, and the pastor was called to the lieutenant's office.

"Did I hear you preaching to the men?" the lieutenant wanted to know.

"Yes," the prisoner confessed, "that is true."

"What were you talking about?"

"I was preaching the gospel of Jesus Christ."

"You said something about joy and how we can find it. I want you to tell me about that."

The surprised pastor related again the way to salvation — and the resultant joy — through faith in Christ. He was even more surprised to hear the lieutenant ask, "Is it possible for me to have this joy?" Soon the men were praying together.

The lieutenant resigned his commission and suffered abuse at the hands of the State, but he became a loyal Christian witness.

It is to such lovers of freedom that Fernandez' broadcasts lend encouragement. Had he stayed in Cuba, he would never have lived to reach his present widespread audience with the old-yet-new message of hope.

*Smiles of relief and triumph, as another group
safely completes the crossing of the 90-mile
corridor between oppression and opportunity.*
7th U.S. Coast Guard District official photo

# Chapter Eight

# GOING OR STAYING-PRAYING

The needs of the oppressed people of Cuba speak clearly through the true stories in the preceding pages: freedom to worship, to evangelize, and to train their children; equality of opportunity for jobs and education; and justice in the courts. Cubans, Christians and non-Christians, need the prayers of God's people around the world.

Cubans are now a scattered people. Estimates of the number of Cuban emigrants vary from 500,000 to a million. The majority have come to the United States, either directly on American-sponsored freedom flights or on escape vessels, or indirectly through Spain, Mexico, and Central America. A number have found refuge in other parts of the world.

These Cubans sacrifice virtually every material possession — and sometimes risk death from water-front guards or a hostile sea — to find freedom. The Christians depart their homeland after much soul-searching, and as refugees they face bewildering problems. In America, as elsewhere, they find sympathy and assistance, for which they are extremely grateful, but the transition to a new life is painful.

Refugees experience fear and uncertainty as they arrive in a new country where they must register, have their passports validated, receive inoculations and vaccinations, and be subjected to hours of questioning. Then they face the adjustment to a new environment and often a new language. While many coming to the United States settle in the protective confines of "Little Cuba" in Miami, immersed in the language, customs, and culture of their old country, they still don't feel at home. One new resident, in her first encounter with an American supermarket, discovered cans of "tuna" at a bargain price. Only at the checkout counter did she learn that what she had picked up for her family was cat food.

The U.S. government and church and charitable organizations offer assistance to the refugees, but of necessity it is limited. Cubans are self-sufficient people and strive to take care of their own. It takes a while for a new refugee to get on his feet, but most of them make it. Some do surprisingly well. Several Cuban-managed Miami businesses boast a million-dollar annual turnover.

Successful or otherwise, Cubans encounter a certain amount of prejudice from Americans and a disconcerting condescension. Their opinions are sometimes rejected simply because they are "non-

American." Under such social strictures, refugees take a long time to feel at home.

Christians among the refugees have displayed an amazing contentment nonetheless. They characteristically explain their serenity by affirming their conviction that God, who brought them to a free land, will one day guide them back to Cuba — or build their lives anew in a strange country. Their hope is grounded in the sovereign will of God, not the maneuverings of nations.

And they seek the fellowship and prayer support of God's people in their new homeland.

Of course, many Cubans have chosen to remain in their homeland. Brother Andrew, whose report of his visits to Cuba appears at the beginning of this book, encouraged Cuban Christians to stay on the island. He urged them to reconsider their role as Christian citizens: "Is it to run — or is it to stand?" Andrew knew that life in Cuba was not easy, but he reasoned: "Perhaps God has a purpose for putting you in this place at this time. Perhaps you are to be his legs and his arms and his healing hands in this situation."

In one of Brother Andrew's meetings a man stood up and told the group, "I am a Methodist minister. For the last few years I have worked as a barber [to gain enough money to feed a large family], but God has spoken to me this evening. I am going to return to the ministry."

Joyous shouts of "Gracias, Pastor!" echoed through the room.

A couple who were due to fly out within two weeks told Brother Andrew they were turning in their treasured airline tickets. "From now on Cuba is our mission field," they said.

Such people also need the prayers of Christians in free lands.

There is yet another urgent prayer concern on the lips of Christian refugees. It may seem unrelated to their special problems, but it is prompted by bitter memories of their native land. They remember the successive stages of upheaval that shook and re-shaped their island home, and now they look apprehensively at the turmoil in America: the Communist infiltration of education and labor groups, the outbreak of revolutionary activity in the cities, the student conflicts, the societal confusion.

Cuban Christians are very much aware of the threat these forces pose. That's why they pray fervently — and urge the prayers of fellow-believers — not only for Cuba's deliverance from oppression but also for America's preservation of freedom.

They know what it means to lose it.

## CUBAN CONVULSIONS

1492 — DISCOVERY
> On October 28, 1492, Christopher Columbus claimed the island for Spain.

1895 — INDEPENDENCE STRUGGLE
> Jose Marti (Cuba's George Washington) led a revolt in 1895. American sympathy went to the rebels.

1898 — AMERICAN INTERVENTION
> The sinking of the U.S.S. *Maine* in Havana Harbor on February 15, 1898, precipitated the four-month Spanish-American War (April-August). The signing of the Treaty of Paris on December 10 ended Cuba's 400-year colonial status.

1901 — CONSTITUTION ADOPTED
> The Platt Amendment to Cuba's constitution, which was adopted in 1901, gave the United States the right of intervention in Cuban internal affairs.

## 1934 — ENTER BATISTA

President Franklin D. Roosevelt, originator of the Good Neighbor Policy, signed a treaty nullifying the Platt Amendment in 1934. In this same year Fulgencio Batista y Zaldivar started the first of his two Cuban dictatorships. It lasted ten years, then his candidate was defeated electorally in 1944. An army coup just before the 1952 elections restored Batista to power.

## 1953 — "THE TWENTY-SIXTH OF JULY MOVEMENT"

Student revolutionary Fidel Castro Ruz led an abortive raid against a Cuban army barracks on July 26, 1953. A hundred rebels lost their lives and Castro was imprisoned, but the date became a rallying cry for Cuban revolutionaries. Castro was released in 1954 and went into exile to organize further revolt.

## 1956 — CIVIL WAR

Castro led another revolt in 1956. Though repulsed, he fled to the Sierra Maestra Mountains at the southern tip of Cuba to engage in guerrilla warfare. Late in 1958 large-scale civil war broke out.

## 1959 — CASTRO VICTORY

Premier Batista fled Cuba on New Year's Day, 1959. Within six weeks Fidel Castro became Premier. Later in the year Castro launched a purge of anticommunists. By the end of 1960 the Castro government had taken over all businesses and nationalized American-owned industry.

## 1961 — THE BAY OF PIGS

Three months after the United States and Cuba severed diplomatic relations, patriots trained in America and Guatemala failed in an attempt on April 17, 1961, to invade Cuba at the Bay of Pigs. Prisoners were later ransomed by the United States. In December 1961 Castro proclaimed Cuba a socialist state.

## 1962 — MISSILE CRISIS

Cuba's economic alignment with the Communist bloc could not offset the effects of a total U.S. embargo in 1962. Stringent rationing had to be introduced when sugar crops on the collectivized farms were deficient. More frustration came in October when Russia bowed to U.S. demands to remove Soviet missiles from Cuba. The United States, meanwhile, refused Castro's order to give up its naval base at Guantanamo Bay on Cuba's southern coast.

## 1965 — FREEDOM FLIGHTS

Among the few openings that have been made in the "sugarcane curtain" since Fidel Castro established his Communist regime was an agreement in 1965 permitting American sponsored airlifts to Miami. By 1969 an estimated half-million Cubans had squeezed through this and other corridors to political freedom.

## 1970 — SUBMARINE SCARE

Tensions between the United States and the Soviet bloc were heightened in the fall of 1970 after the White House warned against building of a Russian submarine base in Cuba. Reminiscent of the 1962 missile crisis, Soviet-American rhetoric was heated before the situation eventually cooled.

## 1971 — POLICE STATE

Dictator Castro rules with a carrot in one hand and a whip in the other, offering free medical care and education to all, and enforcing his decrees through some two million neighborhood spies, members of CDR. While the poor masses revel in their new advantages, 10,000 "enemies of the State" languish in prison and scores of thousands await official permission to abandon their possessions and flee their homeland.